CHURCHILL

Churchill

ISBN-13: 978-1944540371
ISBN-10: 1944540377

For information about production rights, e-mail:
jazzyron@gmail.com

Published by Sordelet Ink

SØRDELET
ink

CHURCHILL

ADAPTED AND WRITTEN BY
RONALD KEATON

INSPIRED FROM THE WRITINGS OF
WINSTON CHURCHILL

THE TELEPLAY BY
DR. JAMES C. HUMES
AND OTHER WRITINGS, WITH GRATITUDE

SORDELET
Ink

CHURCHILL WAS FIRST PERFORMED AT
THE GREENHOUSE THEATER CENTER IN CHICAGO
ON AUGUST 1, 2014 WITH THE FOLLOWING CAST AND CREW:

CHURCHILL .... RONALD KEATON

DIRECTOR....................................KURT JOHNS
SET/LIGHTING................................JASON EPPERSON
SOUND......................................ERIC BACKUS
PROJECTIONS................................PAUL DEZIEL
COSTUME....................................ALICE BROUGHTON
PROPERTIES.................................LYNN DONOVAN
AEA STAGE MANAGER......................JASON SHIVERS

CHURCHILL OPENED AT NEW WORLD STAGES
OFF-BROADWAY IN NEW YORK CITY ON FEBRUARY 6, 2015
WITH THE FOLLOWING CAST AND CREW:

CHURCHILL .... RONALD KEATON

DIRECTOR .... KURT JOHNS
SET/LIGHTING....................................JASON EPPERSON
SOUND ....ERIC BACKUS
PROJECTIONS ....PAUL DEZIEL
COSTUME..ALICE BROUGHTON
PROPERTIES.......................................LYNN DONOVAN
AEA STAGE MANAGER ....JASON SHIVERS

CHURCHILL UNDERSTUDY ....JOHN O'CREAGH

APPRECIATION

TINA SALAMONE
DAVID RICE
MICHAEL COCO
ROBERT SCHNEIDER
DR. JAMES C. HUMES
LEE POLLOCK
THE CHURCHILL CENTRE
SoloChicago Theatre

AND TO THE MUSE FOR IT ALL...

Setting

A LECTURE HALL IN 1946

ACT I

(We hear an old English music hall song - "Champagne Charlie", which continues as the lights ease up, slightly muted and warm on a man sitting in front of a canvas and easel, painting. Small table with colored paints. Palette and brushes. The music fades out. WINSTON CHURCHILL takes a drink and pauses)

CHURCHILL
(Painting as he speaks) This may be the only activity in my life that I actually conduct in silence - painting in oils. Now understand - I don't disparage watercolors one bit. It's just that for me, oil painting is so much easier for correcting one's mistakes. The canvas is for me what golf or tennis is for many others. I enjoyed polo as a younger man for years. But painting...

It concentrates the hand and eye and so relaxes the mind. And I only do landscapes. Very few portraits. Trees and ponds never complain. One sweep of the palette and you lift the veil of tears that were morning's labor; you can make a fresh start. And the colors are so delicious to look at! Matching them is so absorbing.

(Stops painting to address the audience directly)

But I must tell you... I began this painting lark a long time ago as a young, energetic man of 40 at the dawn of the first world war. And on that occasion when my fortunes were at a low ebb - something that happens to me from time to time - the muse of painting suddenly came to me and said "Might these toys be of use to you? They amuse some people." But how to begin. The empty canvas gleamed white before me. The brush hung poised, my hand suspended. The sky that day was blue - the skies are sometimes blue in England - so I carefully mixed a little blue paint with a little white paint. With infinite precaution, I made a mark about the size of a bean on the affronted white canvas.

At that moment, the sound of an approaching motor car halted further actions. And from that vehicle stepped the painter-wife of the great English artist Sir John Lavery.

"What are you doing?" she cried.

"Painting" I said.

"Painting? Then why are you hesitating? Here! Give me a brush! A big one!"

(Faces the canvas)

SPLASH! Into the turpentine! WALLOP! Into the blue and white! A frantic flourish into the palette! And then several large, fierce strokes and slashes upon the positively shivering canvas! Anyone could see that it could not fight back. The spell in me was broken.

I saw the canvas grin in helplessness before me. Seizing that largest brush, I fell upon my victim with fury, and I haven't had awe of a canvas since.

(Returns to easel and sits)

Now you see, with watercolor, I could never turn this from an English landscape to champagne and caviar...or could I?

(Looking at painting)

Painting is an unending discovery for me. I hope you'll take the time to try it before you die.

(Fade out to blue as sound of Truman introducing CHURCHILL leads to applause. A 'speaking engagement', which is actually an informal gathering of a great many people. A large table, with chairs on both ends, sits center stage. On the table are an ashtray, a glass and a pitcher of water. In the back on the wall are the Stars and Stripes and the Union Jack. A winged chair sits stage left, the easel stage right. CHURCHILL enters, hat in hand, with a cane. Flashes "V" sign)

CHURCHILL

Thank you, thank you...your welcome warms my heart! Not for the first time have I come running to America in search of comfort, as a child would seek its mother. And when you are being introduced by the President of the United States, it's a world forum. How do you resist? I am happy to be here with you on this wonderful occasion. Many times, I have been welcomed in your country, and that of your great neighbor, Canada. And I've never failed to be stimulated by the experience. Why shouldn't I love you Yanks? After all, my father married one!

Excuse me...She wasn't a Yank. She was a Dodger, born in Brooklyn!

(Puts cane on table before crossing behind it)

There we are; that's how it begins. That's how most families begin, I suppose - with a young man falling in love with a pretty girl. No superior alternative has yet been found. In my case, it begins with the son of a British duke falling in love with an American beauty. My mother was an American...Jenny Jerome. And ancestors of mine were officers in Washington's army. So I am myself a kind of English-speaking union. I came miraculously into the world with a certain amount of impatience and with a good deal of energy. At 1:30 o'clock in the morning on the 30th of November, 1874 in a tiny bedroom of a very big house, Blenheim Palace, the home of my grandfather, the Duke of Marlborough.

I should have been born in London - that was the plan. But my mother and father had been invited down to Blenheim Palace for the weekend, and I fear my 20-year-old mother may have precipitated the birth by over-activity. I was born six weeks premature. Nothing was prepared for so momentous an occasion. No baby clothes. Everything had to be borrowed from the wife of the local doctor. There's no doubt that I was over-punctual for that first appointment in my life - a habit, I fear, I have not continued. I do, don't you, think unpunctuality is a vile thing. I've tried to break myself of it all my life, but I fear I've developed a tiresome habit of missing trains and planes. But then, as my wife says: I am a sporting man; I like to give them a fair chance of getting away.

I can see my mother now in misty memories of my nineteenth century childhood. At Vice Regal Lodge in Dublin, where my grandfather was, by then, viceroy. You see, in those days, Ireland was a dominion of Great Britain. I see her receiving guests, a lithe, dark figure − radiant, translucent, intense. The diamond pin in her hair only dimmed by the flashing glory of her eyes. One of her admirers likened her to a panther. To me, she shone like the evening star - brilliant, but remote.

My father, Lord Randolph Churchill, was a somewhat austere man, a brilliant politician. He had a fierce pride, which sometimes led him into stormy waters. It was as a result of an altercation with the Prince of Wales that he'd been banished to Ireland to serve as secretary to his father, the Duke. I fear that as a boy I was somewhat of a disappointment to my father. And my congenital lisp and stutter didn't help, to be sure. I would he'd lived to see the turn in my fortunes. He adored my mother. I can see them now as they were, together in Ireland...he, as they rode to the hunt, tall and majestic in the saddle... she, in a riding habit that fitted her like a skin, often beautifully spattered with mud.

(Crosses to easy chair)

The woman I was closest to in my childhood was my nanny, Mrs. Everest. Little Ella, the daughter of a clergyman from Cumberland. I called her "Womany". She was my confidante. She, it was, who looked after me and tended all my needs. It was to her that I poured out my many troubles. I mourn her passing to this very day. Death came easily to her. She'd lived such an innocent and loving life in service to others that she had no fears at all and did not seem to mind dying very much. She'd been my dearest and most intimate companion for all of the first twenty years that I'd lived. When I think of the fate of poor old women, some of whom have no one to look after them and nothing to live on at the end of their days, I'm proud to have had a hand in all that structure of pensions and insurance, which is so especially helpful to them. If there be any, as I trust there may be some, who rejoice that I lived, then it is to my favorite friend and excellent woman, Elizabeth Everest, that their gratitude is due.

The really unhappy years of my life were in my school days.

(Crosses behind table)

You see, I was sent away to boarding school at the age of seven. My mother's heart was not centered in the nursery, and I never could please my father very much. At school, my rebellious spirit seemed at odds with what I often thought were unnecessary disciplines. The floggings... My first school, I had the great misfortune to become the victim of a truly sadistic headmaster - a young man who seemed to make punishment of his students a hobby to enjoy, who died early of a heart attack, brought on, it was said, by over activity with the cane. It was in retaliation for one of his beatings that I incurred further wrath by kicking his Sunday straw hat to pieces!

At the end of my first term, I was placed in a class of eleven. When I was at home, Womany would tuck me in bed and read a poem to me. But at school, of course, there was no Womany, no poem at bedtime. So

I would hide a book of verses underneath the basin in the common lavatory and seek moments during the day when I could memorize a poem. At night in one of the eight little beds in my dormitory, I would recite myself to sleep. Rolling those remembered words off my tongue gave rise for me to one of the greatest structures in God's creation - the cadence of an English sentence. I'm still biased in favor of boys learning English. I let the clever ones learn Latin as an honor and Greek as a treat.

But the one thing I'd whip 'em for is not knowing English - I'd whip 'em hard for that! I'd punish no child who was slow in mathematics. Few were slower than I was. I found it all very perplexing. The figures were tied together in all sorts of tangles, and they did things to one another. It was all extremely difficult to forecast.

The only prize I ever won was for a poetry reading as my next school, Harrow. An establishment of some note − principally perhaps because Byron, the great poet, was there. Before me. This prize I won at the age of fourteen was for reciting twelve hundred lines from Thomas McCauley's Lays Of Ancient Rome. I still remember most of them:

"For the great man helped the poor man
And the poor man loved the great.
Then none was for the party
And all was for the state...."

(Looks at the audience) Well, I'll spare you the rest.

(Retrieves cigar from table)

I so wanted my father to come and hear me. But he never visited me. You want to know how many conversations I had with my father over a lifetime? Maybe five. One morning I was in my nursery, playing with my toy soldiers, when to my great surprise and delight, the door opened and Father came in. After a while he said, "Winston... would you like to be a soldier?" "Yes, Papa." I thought he had sensed in me some semblance of military genius!

After all, what else could a descendant of the great Duke of Marlborough say? In those days, a boy of my upbringing had only four choices of career: the land, the law, the church or the military. And as I later heard my father say to my mother "Well, Jenny, the boy has no land, he's too stupid for the law, he's too obstreperous for the clergy - " so it was the military for me.

The night before the entrance exams at

Sandhurst, the equivalent of your West Point -- I took them three times, by the way -- I studied hard for the geography question, which carried twenty points. I clipped the names of all the British dominions out of an atlas and put them in a hat. I closed my eyes and pulled one out. It was New Zealand. I drew it over and over again. The next morning, the examining officer wrote the first question on the blackboard: Draw a map of New Zealand. It was like breaking the bank at Monte Carlo. I not only sketched the country perfectly, I put in the railroads, the bridges, the canals, the libraries, the parks. I got all twenty points. Couple that with the history essay that I wrote, I thus squeaked into Sandhurst.

I enjoyed my early training there and developed a certain reputation for resourcefulness and the instinct for command, following an incident with a much-prized gift from my father - a gold watch. I was walking along the lake at Sandhurst; I bent down to pick up a stick. My watch fell from my pocket and plunged into the deepest water. Despite repeated efforts to retrieve it by diving into the lake, I couldn't find it. I was utterly miserable. But I assembled a detachment of fellow cadets and had them dig a new channel to divert the stream that fed the lake. Then I commandeered the Sandhurst fire engine and pumped that lake dry. I found the watch and I refilled the lake.

Those toy soldiers from childhood changed my path. Real life had at last begun. Graduated eighth in my class, a royal accomplishment for me, indeed for any young man...which still did not placate Lord Randolph. I tried so hard. So hard. I realized with time I was not the easiest child to parent. But my parents seemed never to be satisfied. I didn't want solely to be a soldier, no. There was too much of life to explore; I was impatient. I wanted to be a politician like my father, but I couldn't, because I had no money. In those days, Parliament paid no salary... *(Mocking)* What??? The grandson of a duke - no money? Yes, you see, my father was a younger son. It was the eldest son, my uncle, who inherited the estates, the dukedom, Blenheim Palace.

1895. I finally entered my twenty-first year. There was a quick first trip as a military observer to Cuba, where we were chasing rebels, where I picked up two lifetime habits -- cigars and siestas. And soon I was assigned to India. For twenty years. That wasn't a service, it was a life sentence. And my father?

(Stands behind easy chair)

My father had just died at the age of 45... so young. All my dreams of comradeship, of entering Parliament at his side and in his support, went with him. There remained for me only to pursue his aims and vindicate his memory. The rest of my life (and this is not easy for me to admit), I not only chased his shadow; I had this vision that I would even die on the same day - January 24.

But back then, all I could see was ending my life as a forgotten captain in some lost garrison in British India east of nowhere. I remember writing to a young lady:

"Curse ruthless time! Curse our mortality! How cruelly short is the allotted span, for all we must cram into it. We are all worms. But I do believe that I am a glowworm."

So I developed an escape plan. I would seek adventure, find glory and write about it for profit. As I said to my mother: "How many soldiers can put subject and predicate together?" Soon after I arrived for my first duty at Bangalore in India where there was a rebellion, some three thousand miles north on the border with Afghanistan - in those days, India was a vital member of the Empire - I applied for vacation leave and volunteered, all in my first week. I had a chance to go out on a search-and-destroy mission. I was separated from my company. There I was, in a scene not unlike your Wild West movies. Pistol in hand, surrounded by the Indians - the INDIAN Indians - I gunned my way out, rejoined the company and rediscovered something from Cuba: there is nothing more exhilarating in life than to be shot at...without result! I went back to my garrison and wrote a book, a bestseller. And in your country, too.

Then there occurred another war in the Sudan. More fighting, more trouble for us, the British...a world power carries grave disadvantages at times, does it not? Well, the commander-in-chief of the British forces in the Sudan was Lord Kitchener, our greatest soldier. My mother, by writing to some of her friends, managed to wrangle me a position on Lord Kitchener's staff. Now I'm quite certain that the commander-in-chief was not overjoyed at the prospect of a cocky, red-haired lieutenant who had written a book highly critical of the army. I had said that one of the fascinating things about the British Army was the extraordinary number of its generals. Anyway, somehow or another, I found myself attached to a very grand regiment, the 21st Lancers.

Not altogether to their delight, either.

You see, I carried in my other pocket, as it were, a commission from the Morning Post newspaper in London to send accounts of whatever action I might see at 15 pounds sterling a column. Not the sort of thing one was expected to do in the 21st Lancers.

The enemy was sighted near Omdurman. Because my horse was fresh, I was assigned to reconnoiter, find Lord Kitchener and make my report. And thus it was that I finally came face-to-face with the great man. Well, not exactly face-to-face... for I cantered up alongside him, as he rode amid the banners at the head of his army and told him all I'd seen. He asked how far away they were, and how much time he'd got. I made a rapid calculation and said "Sir, certainly an hour... possibly an hour and a half." As he rode away, I kept saying to myself "God, I hope I got it right."

And so I went on my first cavalry charge. The enemy wielded not only guns and spears, but double-edged razor-sharp swords, with which they were extremely proficient. They'd acquired the nickname from our boys of "whirling dervishes", for the way they would strike out at you. So we charged twice into the lines of those whirling dervishes. Officers to the left and right of me were hacked to death...

But still, I survived. How? I don't know. But I did know that I apparently had another role to play in God's plan.

After my book about the Sudan, I finally had the capital to do what I wanted to do all along - enter politics. I resigned my commission and in stood for a seat in Parliament. From the industrial county of Lancastershire, the town of Oldham. I had to run twice in two years. The first time, they wouldn't even take the time to get to know me. The second time, they'd apparently heard all about me and said "Vote him in and get him out of here! I was canvassing a particular area when a young man roared up and exclaimed "Vote for you? Why, I'd rather vote for the Devil!" I said "I understand, sir. But in case your friend isn't running, may I count on your support???

(CHURCHILL turns to table chair and sits. Pours water, taking his time)

I am so happy to be here with you all! America is like a second home to me. Reminds me of my American mother.

(A quick drink)

Now there was news when my parents married. You see, Anglo-American marriages were very rare in those days. I'm afraid the English regarded you American women as a bit of a cross between a red Indian and a gaiety theatre showgirl. Indeed, my mother often said the highest compliment she could receive was "I should never have thought you were an American!"

(Another drink)

When I was a very young man, I did entertain a certain interest in Miss Ethel Barrymore, the fine actress and sister of John and Lionel. And I believe for just a moment, Miss Barrymore may have considered me. But she felt that my world, which was the world of politics, was not for her, so common sense prevailed. And then there was another young lady...and now look here, I believe we're sailing into deep waters. We should probably return to the safe harbor of the House of Commons!

(Sound of a gavel)

The dawn of the new century saw the sun finally set on the long reign of Queen Victoria. In February 1901, I made my oath to Edward VII and took my seat as a duly elected member of the Conservative Party in the House of Commons beside men who had sat with Benjamin Disraeli, William Gladstone and yes, my own father, Lord Randolph Churchill. I tried to look like my father. I wore his polka-dot bowties. I fingered his gold watch chain. I even tried to grow a mustache like his, but unfortunately, my sandy, sparse hair was not equal to the task. A female acquaintance of mine, one of those plutocrats who claimed to love the working man - indeed, they love to see him work -- said to me "Mr. Churchill, I care for neither your politics nor your mustache!" I said "Don't distress yourself, dear lady, you're not very likely to come in contact with either!"

I might wear my father's bowties and watch chain, but I could not put on his brilliance. Lord Randolph was a "first" at Oxford. That's like your Phi Beta Kappa. I was no first. I didn't even went to college, I couldn't get in. And Lord Randolph was a brilliant orator, whose words with little preparation fell into place like jewels on a tiara. On one of the first occasions I spoke

in the House of Commons, I fainted. And
then, as I told you, there was that infernal
lisp and stutter, which occasioned much
mock and ridicule both at school and at
Sandhurst.

At the age of nineteen, I'd gone to a
celebrated oral surgeon, Dr. Felix Simon.
He attended all the great opera singers –
Caruso and the like. I said to him "Please
cure this impediment in my speech. I'm
going into the army now, but I mean to be a
politician later on, and I cannot be haunted
the rest of my days by avoiding every word
that begins with an 's'." Sir Felix said "My
dear boy, an operation is most totally out
of the question, and I strongly advise you
to avoid any occupation or trade in which
speaking is a necessary part of making a
living!" I persevered. If I was inadequate
as a speaker, I determined that one day I
would be accomplished. And despite being
a poor speaker as a youth, I can tell you I
vastly admired my best friend who was a
great orator – David Lloyd-George, who
one day was destined to be prime minister.
I said of David in 1902 in a phrase that
has since become trite: "David can charm
the birds off the trees." He charmed me
across the floor of the House of Commons.
I turned my back on the Conservative

Party and joined his Liberal Party. And
there we were, this unlikely pair, the son
of a Welsh coal miner and the son of an
English aristocrat. Together we crafted
legislation which, a quarter-century later,
your President Roosevelt incorporated
into his "New Deal".

But for doing so, it was not only David who
suffered the "slings and arrows" of right-
wing abuse. You see, like Roosevelt, I was
regarded as a traitor to my class. And like
Roosevelt, I relished the attacks. But the
passions for social reform began to cool in
the shadows of the impending world war. I
was appointed First Lord of the Admiralty.
It was like a captain being given his first
ship. We converted the fleet from coal to
oil. We built the first military aircraft ever
to be used by the Royal Navy. We scrapped
the dinosaurs - that's what I called those
huge battleships - for speedier vessels. Of
course, not all the admirals greeted these
changes with whole-hearted enthusiasm. I
can hear them now: "Sir! You're scuttling
the traditions of the Royal Navy!"
"Admiral, have you ever considered what
the traditions of the Royal Navy really are?
I can tell you in three words: rum, sodomy
and the lash!"

All right, that's five words. But I do love words.

There was the British war bond rally. Don't remember where in the States, but they were serving champagne and fried chicken. It was hosted by a Miss Annabelle Throckmorton. She was a lovely young belle whose endowment for motherhood was doubly manifest. I like people to say what they mean in a straight-forward manner! She offered me the plate of chicken. I said "Thank you, I'll have some breast!" "Mr. Churchill!" she exclaimed. "You mind! Nice folk in Richmond don't use that word. We call it 'white meat'!" The next day, I sent her a corsage and a card that said "Thank you for yesterday. I'd be much honored if you'd pin this on your white meat."

(Sits. Pours Scotch)

And then began, in August 1914, that terrible war against Germany and her allies which cost so many millions of lives...and which was so foolishly called the "war to end all wars". As First Lord of the Admiralty, I labored hard. Even Lord Kitchener said "Well, Winston, no one can say you didn't have the Fleet ready." But if the British Navy was ready, the Army and her people were not. The Army thought it would be all

over in a year; I knew differently. I warned
in a memorandum that Germany would
invade France through Belgium, and that
the war would last four or five years. Alas,
I was right. I usually avoid prophesying
beforehand. It's much better policy to
do so after the event has already taken
place. Indeed, among the most important
qualifications for politics are the ability to
foretell what might happen tomorrow, next
week, next month or next year...AND the
agility to explain afterward why it didn't
happen.

I had two ideas to shorten the war.

One was a design for a landship. We had to
put a stop to our boys getting hung up in
the barbed wire in France and facing the
dreaded machine gun fire in the trenches.
The general staff called my landship
"Winston's folly". Today it is known as
the tank. It greatly reduced casualities and
helped to end trench warfare. But if my
first idea was a triumph, the second was a
tragedy - the Dardenelles. I thought that
Turkey, Germany's ally, could be knocked
out of the war quickly. At my instigation,
the British Navy steamed up the Dardenelle
Straits and did their job of bombardment.
But Lord Kitchener held the Army back

until it was a case of too little, too late. The Germans had already reinforced the heights. Our boys were slaughtered on the Gallipoli Peninsula. How I was hated back home. My political career was over.

(Lights shift to a single pool, into which CHURCHILL walks. The sound of men arguing. CHURCHILL in discussion)

"They only want me out. I hear the voices all around me, feel them through me. The ghosts of the Gallipoli dead never simply a memory, but an albatross. A black dog of depression crawling inside me like an infection! And it was my fault???"

(The sound of a heavy door slam)

"I am not irrelevant!"

(Lights slowly restore)

I left those politics and went to join the fight in France. Because of my rank, eventually I was given a battalion and went to fight on the Western front. One day, it was my usual duty to make a routine visit to headquarters. On this day, I didn't want to go; I didn't want to leave my men. But my colonel insisted and after some argument, away I went. At that moment, a bomb obliterated the very spot where I was standing. Well, there you are, you see. How could I not believe that destiny had once again, in the nick of time, extended its hand and saved me? So in November 1918, after you people had joined us as comrades-in-arms, that grievous, bloody, pitiless war came to an end.

In the early days of peace, Prime Minister Lloyd-George rescued me from political oblivion and made me one of his Secretaries of State. "Winston" he said, "We have ten months to end the bloody conflicts in Ireland and the Middle East."

"David, you're asking me to do in a year what kings, saints, prophets and diplomats have failed to do in a thousand." Well, the first step, I felt, was a Jewish homeland. I'd felt for years that the noble vision of a promised land must be fulfilled under a flag of tolerance and freedom. As for Ireland, we in Britain were quite decided – Well, you know, we have always regarded the Irish to be a trifle odd. You see, they refuse to be English, especially their brilliant advocate for the Irish Free State, Michael Collins.

In our challenging negotiations at my Chartwell home, Collins took it personally: "You hunted me down, Churchill; you put a price on my head!" I said to him "Look up there, sir!" Pointing to a framed copy of the reward for my re-capture in South Africa. "At least you drew a good price - 5000 pounds. Look at this – '25 pounds, dead or alive' – how would you like that??" Thankfully, Collins laughed. Michael Collins was a visionary, as my responsibility was to preserve the Empire. We were always at odds, always fighting. But remember. I understood his Gaelic passion.

So despite Irish independence, despite the Jewish settlement in Palestine - or perhaps because of those two treaties - the Liberal Party was wiped off the political map by the Socialist Party, led by Ramsey MacDonald, a Scot. Now I have nothing against Scots; I married one. But Mr. MacDonald was a Calvinist. A pacifist. A teetotaler. He had, more than any other man, the remarkable gift of compressing the largest amount of words into the smallest amount of thought.

(Crosses to chair and sits)

I listened to the news of that election while in hospital, having an operation for appendicitis. So there I was. Without a ministry. Without a party. Without a seat. And without an appendix...

(Opens a box on the table)

When I travel, I carry dozens of letters of correspondence with me, so I might answer them as time permits. Let me share one with you. From a marvelous young man in Boston Massachusetts. He began his letter "Dear Mr. Prime Minister". He explained that his father had fought in the Third Army and heard me often on the radio. He didn't think much of me until he discovered we keep race horses. Now I'm his favorite Limey! Yes, but do they win many races? Short answer - no. I had one horse that showed great promise. Colonist II, I called him. I thought he was going to win the Derby. I had a serious talk with him before that race. I said "If you win this race, you'll spend the rest of your days in extremely agreeable female company." Came in fourth - couldn't keep his mind on the race!

And he had a question: "Mr. Churchill, what do you think was your greatest speech?" My greatest speech. Lor...

(Sound of thunder and lightning, followed by a steady rain. Lights shift to a night glow as CHURCHILL moves chair and sits)

I was walking hand-in-hand with a Miss Clementine Hozier on the grounds of Blenheim Palace. In our first meeting at a social gathering, I took note of her personal grace and beauty. Our second meeting convinced me that here was a woman of great character and intelligence, and I fell in love almost instantly. We'd seen a short courtship, maybe nine months. During our walk, a sudden rainstorm forced us to take shelter. And there I asked for her hand. My audience of one. It must have been my greatest speech – she said yes. A couple of days later, she wrote me a note: "I don't know how I have lived these twenty-three years without you." We wrote her mother for her hand and, upon her approval, we were married on September 12, 1908. And we lived happily ever after...

(Sound of storm rises, then disappears)

I call her "Pussycat" and she calls me "Pig". Sometimes when I get home, I'll shout "Oink! Oink!" And she'll reply "Meow! Meow!" if she feels like it. Once during the war, we were on all fours under the dinner table with our adult children, all of us oinking and meowing, when suddenly in walked the Archbishop of Canterbury. He was somewhat surprised. Another time at dinner with the same Archbishop and the Lord Chancellor, we were each asked if we could not be who we were, who we would most like to be. When it came my turn, I said "If I could not be who I am, I think I should most like to be Mrs. Churchill's second husband."

We had five children. One of them, a baby girl Marigold, died in 1921. General Eisenhower told me he'd lost a baby son, Dwight Dowd, at about that same time. There's Randolph, who followed the professions of his father - journalism and politics - with mixed results; Sarah, who chose what many people say is my true profession - acting; and Diana and Mary, each of whom followed their mother's example and married a politician...Different ones, to be sure...There's a dinner with the Archbishop, eh? Clementine thinks that I am too permissive a parent, but if I do indulge my children, it's because my parents largely ignored me. I had one golden rule: Do what you like, but remember - like what you do.

(The faint sound of chimes up, then fade out. Lights return to lecture hall. CHURCHILL crosses to table)

Well, there I was, out of office again. There was nothing for me to do but go home. I had ample private time. I was painting and writing. The History of the First World War.

With my own hands, I helped in building a cottage. And an extensive garden wall. I designed and built the waterworks for my collection of goldfishes. I was made a member of the bricklayers' union...

You don't believe any of this, do you? Well, you'll simply have to come one day to Chartwell, my home, and I'll show it all to you. There's something very reassuring about laying bricks, you know. Everything has to be straight. Regular. Orderly. Qualities I greatly admire in all of life's endeavors. One day at Chartwell, I asked my dear friend and scientific advisor, Professor Frederick Lindemann, how long it would take me to finish my wall. I gave him all the details of height and length and so on. I told him I could lay a brick a minute...a brick a minute. The Prof got out his slide rule, made some computations and said it would take me at least fifteen years. 1939. I said "Lor, I'll be dead by then!"

See what I mean about prophecy?

That same year 1924 saw the Socialists still in power. But there was another election coming, and I felt able to offer myself to the people again. You know, I'll wager that I've been involved in more elections than anyone in history - fourteen of them.

Won my share. By now, I had rejoined the Conservative Party because I felt there was no longer an effective Liberal Party.

But I despise socialism. It's a philosophy of failure. Its inherent virtue is the equal sharing of misery.

Well, in 1924 we booted out the Socialists. The new Prime Minister, Mr. Stanley Baldwin, asked me to be Chancellor of the Exchequer. A post my father had held some thirty-eight years before. I even wore his same robes, which my mother had carefully put away in mothballs. But after six years of hard labor, the Conservatives were defeated just before the advent of the Great Depression. To tell the truth, I was exhausted.

(The sound of a Hitler speech, low and running under CHURCHILL's speech)

I could hear the stormy rumblings. And that one insistent voice. For seven years, he was a man without a country; he wasn't even German, he was Austrian! Mein Kampf, indeed.

(Hitler's voice fades out)

Britain and the rest of the world stood idly by while Germany was being reborn. But the appeasing Conservatives were no less spineless than the pacifist Socialists. So one day in the House of Commons I told them all this story:

(The sound of the House of Commons gathering. Lights shift to a bright beam, narrowly focused as CHURCHILL walks back and forth downstage)

"When I was a boy, my parents allowed me to go to Barnum's circus. Now there was a collection of freaks and monstrosities, one of which I earnestly desired to see. But my parents hesitated. They thought it was too revolting, too demoralizing for my youthful eye.

It was called 'the boneless wonder'.

After fifty years, I have often wondered what such a thing might be. Well, now I know, because I'm surrounded by them here in this chamber.

(The sound of angry voices fighting)

Ladies and gentlemen - The Boneless Wonders!"

(Lights restore to lecture hall. CHURCHILL ends centerstage)

I was not popular on either side of the House.

In truth, I did feel that I had precious few friends. I was well and truly in the "wilderness" of politics for the next decade. My mood was heavy and dark, that 'black dog' hanging all around me. But I intended to occupy my mind. I had my house and garden at Chartwell. I had my family and my darling Clemmie.

I must be very tough or very lucky. Or both.

Those were hard days before the Second World War. I had a very difficult series of meetings with the German Ambassador to whom I finally said I thought the British government would never agree to giving Hitler a free hand in Eastern Europe. But the Ambassador said: "Then war is inevitable. Nothing will stop him and nothing will stop us."

(Crosses to left chair, sits) We returned to our respective corners.

Well, you can imagine what was next.

(Speaking to empty chair) "Sir. When you speak of war - which no doubt would be general war - you must not underrate England. She's a curious country. Few foreigners can understand her mind. When a great cause is presented to the people, all

kinds of unexpected actions might occur. You plunge us into another war, sir, and the Union Jack will bring the whole world against you like last time!"

But the Ambassador knew that not everyone in England felt as I felt. Among the pacifists, there was, of course, Lady Astor - an American by birth - and her Cliveden set, who all regarded Hitler as a responsible German nationalist - much more responsible than I was in my attacks on the British government for their feeble response to the Nazis. I called Lady Astor and her friends "appeasers". An appeaser is someone who feeds the crocodile, hoping it will feed on him last. Tick-tock, eh? Once after dinner over coffee, after considerable disagreement on the right course for the country, Lady Astor said heatedly to me, straight as an arrow:

"Winston, if you were my husband, I'd put poison in your coffee." I told her "Nancy, if I were your husband, I'd damned well drink it!"

But the policy of the British government continued to be the "crocodile policy". I sometimes think democracy is the worst form of government. Except for every other form that's ever been tried.

(The sound of a single tympani beat)

Then in 1938 came the cruel, unresisted dismemberment of Czechoslovakia.

(Another single tympani beat)

And to a hero's welcome, one of its naive architects, Prime Minister Neville Chamberlain, returned from Munich, hat in hand, proclaiming that we had achieved "peace in our time." I said "Mr. Prime Minister, you had the choice between dishonor and war. You have chosen dishonor..."

(The sound of rising tympani beating)

"...and you will get war!"

(Blackout)

ACT II

(In darkness we hear the BBC newsreel of Chamberlin's announcement of war)

CHAMBERLIN *(V.O.)*
This morning the British Ambassador in Berlin handed the German Government a final Note stating that, unless we heard from them by 11 o'clock that they were prepared at once to withdraw their troops from Poland, a state of war would exist between us.

I have to tell you now that no such undertaking has been received, and that consequently this country is at war with Germany.

(Lights come up full)

CHURCHILL
...and so we got war...

September 1, 1939.

Nazi panzer divisions galloped over the hapless cavalry of helpless Poland. The following spring, Belgium surrendered; the Netherlands fell. French and British armies were being pushed back in France. Europe was at a crossroad; Mr. Chamberlain had been asked to resign. He could not have misjudged Hitler more. And all but one British newspaper had supported him. No one listened to me. Britain finally felt she needed a new leader, one who had seen war, who knew its ferocity and its implacable demands upon men and women and children.

Therefore, His Majesty the King summoned me to Buckingham Palace. His Majesty received me ever so graciously and bade me sit down. He looked at me searchingly for some moments. My road to this moment was nothing if not challenging, and well he knew it. He said quietly "I don't suppose you know why I have sent for you here." Adopting his mood, I replied "Your Majesty, I simply cannot imagine why." He laughed and said "I want to ask you to form a government." I said I certainly would.

A government of national character – that's what was needed in this terrible hour! I told the King that I would try to form a war cabinet of all parties, a coalition government - and a task of dire and somber consequence. No one knew better than I what weaknesses in our preparations lay undisclosed. My warnings in the past had been so numerous and so detailed. And now so terribly vindicated.

But at last, I had been given complete authority over the whole scene. I felt as if I was walking with destiny, and that all my past life had been but preparation for this hour, this trial. I thought I knew a good deal about it all; I was sure I would not fail. And although impatient for the coming dawn, I slept soundly. I had no need for cheering dreams.

Facts are better than dreams. I became prime minister.

They asked me what my program would be. I replied "The only thing I have to offer you is blood, toil, tears and sweat." That same day I took office began the eventual fall of France. Our armies in France were being pushed back to the coast by German tanks and trapped on the beaches at Dunkirk. I told Clemmie that what we needed was a miracle, another Moses who could part the English Channel as he had the Red Sea... for the Nazis, like the Egyptians, were right on their heels.

And we got our miracle - a fog. Under cover of that fog went out from Britain a great fleet of ships and boats, steam and sail, of every shape and size. Every family that had a motorboat or a dinghy or a dory helped the Navy bring those boys home. Crowds. Scattered groups. Sometimes just two or three at a time. It took nine long days, but thousands of our boys were snatched from the ravening clutches of the Nazis and brought home to the white cliffs of their native shores.

And yet even while all that was going on, some even in my own cabinet wanted me to negotiate with the Nazis at home and even abroad. Like your own ambassador Joseph Kennedy, who predicted defeat and counseled surrender. I gave my answer in the House of Commons:

(As he crosses downstage, the sound of the House of Commons returns, and the narrow light with it)

"We shall go on to the end; we shall fight in France; we shall fight on the seas and oceans, we shall fight with growing confidence and growing strength in the air; we shall defend our island, whatever the cost may be. We shall fight on the beaches, we shall fight in the landing grounds, we shall fight in the fields and in the streets, we shall fight in the hills; we shall never surrender!"

(The lights restore as he sits in the chair)

Although there was never a broadcast during the war from the House of Commons, I spoke often to the homefront via radio, much like your famous "Fireside Chats". On one occasion I found myself needing to take a taxi to the BBC studios to deliver an address to the nation at 8:00 PM. As one drew up, the aide gave the cabbie the instructions. The cabbie said "Sorry, guv, I've got to get home to listen to the Prime Minister on my radio!" Of course, I appreciated that. I stuck my head in and handed him a five-pound note - 'I'm in a hurry to get to that address.' Delighted with the five-pound note, the cabbie said "Get in, guv'nor - frig the bloody Prime Minister!" Fame is fleeting at any age, you know.

In those dark days and darker nights, for more than a year we fought on alone. The fighting in France was over in five short weeks. Thus began, in full force, what we called the Battle of Britain. Hitler had decided not to invade us by land, but instead to try and bomb us into defeat. And the bombings were endless. One Sunday afternoon at the Royal Air Force Command Center, there was a huge map on the wall with red buttons representing the Nazi Luftwaffe bombers and blue buttons whenever one of our pilots went up to defend our island. Toward dusk I cried out: "Air Marshall, where are all the blue buttons? There are no more blue buttons!" He replied: "That's because every last plane we have is in the air!" There were no more blue buttons.

Then a young flight commander came in and began to remove the red buttons; the Nazi Luftwaffe had turned tail! They were going home! General Ismay tried to speak to me: "Please. Sir…Never in the field of human conflict was so much owed by so many to so few."

And in those fateful hours - perhaps the finest hours of all our long history - I never lost faith in our survival, because I knew that, in due time, the new world would come to the rescue of the old. I also had an epiphany of sorts that Corporal Hitler, in his lunacy, would turn and invade Russia. I even had warnings sent through neutrals, but Uncle Joe Stalin wouldn't hear of it. After all, Germany was his ally and he had a pact with Hitler to prove it. Then a couple of years later on a Sunday afternoon - things always seem to happen in England on a Sunday afternoon - my chief assistant John Culville told me of the German invasion of Russia. I said "Jock, we must send arms to the Soviet Union!" He said "Prime Minister, how could you, who has always stood against the Bolsheviks and despised communism, send aid to Russia?" "Jock, if Hitler invaded Hell, I would make at least one favorable reference to the devil in the House of Commons."

Hitler - that blood-thirsty guttersnipe, that repositorian example of the most virulent hatred that ever corroded the human breast - had finally ...finally bitten off more than he could chew. And he seemed to have forgotten a lesson that you and I learned in elementary school, that Napoleon discovered in battle: There is a winter in Russia. There is snow and ice. Corporal Hitler must have been very loosely educated.

(Sits)

In December 1941, your special envoy to Britain, Averill Harriman, was in conference with me. I interrupted him and said "I'm sorry Averill, but it's time for the BBC news." And that's when I first heard about the bombings at Pearl Harbor. I immediately called President Roosevelt in Washington. He said, "Well, Winston, we're all in the same boat now." That night, I slept the sleep of the saved and the thankful. God bless America. And made preparations to sail for the States.

Of course, as I've told you, it wasn't my first visit. On my first lecture tour, I was introduced by Mark Twain. I've known every president since McKinley; they all impressed me. But the feeling was not always reciprocated. Teddy Roosevelt, for a time, thought that I was a showoff. Herbert Hoover, with whom I had dealings from the first world war, called me stubborn. And Clemmie even told me . - Well, let's face facts.

(As lights focus on the down left chair, he crosses to sit there for the next speech)

Clementine was the one who kept me anchored. Whenever I showed a bit of arrogance or conceit, she always coached me back to reality. If ever any man owed his wife, it was me. Immeasurably. Early in the war, when the bombing began in London, she cautioned me in a letter:

"My darling, I hope you will forgive me if I tell you something I feel you ought to know. One of the men in your entourage, a devoted friend, has been to me and told me there is a danger of your being generally disliked by your colleagues and subordinates because of your rough, sarcastic and overbearing manner."

She went on: "Winston, I must confess that I have noticed a deterioration in your manner and you are not so kind as you used to be. You will not get the best results by irascibility and rudeness, they will breed either dislike or a slave mentality." My, my. Her eloquence basically said to me "I do hope you will not continue making a further ass of yourself." I've derived continued benefit from criticism in my life and never known any time when I was short of it.

(Lights restore as he crosses to the table)

Thankfully England had one friend still that it could count on, even in darkest times. President Roosevelt and I would exchange, from time to time, our favorite poems of the moment. I still hold close a letter that he sent me when England was in grave peril early in the war. In it he sent a poem from Longfellow that he wrote out in his own hand, saying that it applied to you people as well as us:

"Sail on, O ship of state!
Sail on, O union strong and great!
Humanity with all its fears,
With all the hope of future years
Is hanging breathless on thy fate."

What answer should I give this great man, this thrice-elected leader of one hundred thirty million people?

"Put your confidence in us. Give us your faith and your blessing. And under Providence, all will be well. We shall not fail or falter. We shall not weaken or tire. Neither the sudden shock of battle, nor the long-drawn trials of vigilance or exertion will wear us down. Give us the tools and we will finish the job." And you responded with your generous and invaluable "lend-lease" arrangement.

Two weeks after Pearl Harbor, I arrived in Washington to spend Christmas with the Roosevelt family. It was my first time spending the holidays in America. I fell in love with many of the customs and songs of the season. When I heard those children singing "...the hopes and fears of all the years are met in thee tonight", well, I could have cried with joy like a child at Christmas. And after that, I addressed a joint session of Congress, where I said "If my father were American and my mother English, I might have gotten there on my own.

(He takes off his coat and hangs it on the stage-right chair)

My first morning, your President wheeled into the Monroe Room, just as I was emerging from my bath. As he reversed his path I said "Pray, sir, don't leave. The King's First Minister has nothing to hide from the President of the United States." Meeting President Roosevelt was like opening your first bottle of champagne. And knowing him was like drinking it. He was the best friend England ever had.

(The sound of chimes blowing in the wind, low as the lights focus on the painting area. CHURCHILL crosses to his easel)

You know, the only time that I could really paint during the war was on a trip to Marrakech in 1943, following the conference in Casablanca. I had visited some years earlier and fell in love with the city. I was simply astonished by Morocco, but Marrakech is the loveliest spot in the world. I invited President Roosevelt to come with me to the Mamounia Hotel, where we would ascend the six stories of the Hotel Tower and observe the breathtaking sunset of the Atlas Mountains. After the drive, we discovered that the President's wheelchair wouldn't fit going up the stairs. Talk about being humbled...Now don't get me wrong. I was the one humbled. The President looked at his aides and said "Well, I'm game if you are!" And these two men cradled the President up that winding staircase six floors to the Hotel Tower and then came back down for his things. Arguably the most powerful man in the Western world, and he fought his own physical fraility through the strength of others to conquer that ascent. And the view. It all made me tremble with gratitude. We talked our business. We had dinner. Told stories and sang songs. The next morning at the airport, I resolved to create a remembrance of that visit. And I painted that vista for my friend, the President of the United States. The only one I could finish during the war.

(The sound of chimes grows louder)

You see, painting gives you a new set of eyes. The first quality needed is audacity. Time stands respectfully aside. Whatever the worries of the hour, once the picture has begun to flow along, there is no room for worries in the mental screen. They disappear into shadow and darkness. You have all you need. You. And the canvas. And the world.

(Chimes fade away as lights restore to the lecture hall. CHURCHILL again uses the downstage at his discretion)

Of course all this is not to say that when we became allies in the fullest sense of the word, we did not have our disagreements, as any family would. You had your "Blood and Guts" George Patton. We had Bernard Montgomery. That magnificent soldier. In defeat, unbeatable. In victory, unbearable. And your State Department gentlemen were not always the most helpful. They would follow your Secretary of State's example and became the bull who carried his own china shop around with him.

Then there was General Eisenhower. Yes, we argued, it's true. Especially about the date of the invasion of Normandy. I thought the

Americans were being too precipitous. I said "I have my doubts, I have my doubts." All I could see in my mind's eye were the tides of Normandy running red with the blood of American and British youth. But Eisenhower stuck to his guns. When he said "Like Caesar, we must go forward", I looked at him. And I saw the dilemma of this great general. I said "We are in this with you to the end, sir. And if it fails, we shall all go down together."

Only last year in a meeting with Ike, I shared with him some of my frustrations. I said "You know, the only thing worse than fighting with allies in a time like this is fighting without them!" Then Ike asked me what my greatest problem had been. The real cross we had to bear was the Cross of Lorraine himself, Charles DeGaulle. Now DeGaulle was the very spirit of French resistance and now stands among the world's great leaders. But in those days, he could be difficult. I said "Ike, the problem is that DeGaulle thinks he's Joan of Arc. And the difference is that my bishops won't allow me to burn him!" Well, I didn't burn him, but I did quite often seem to put him in a towering rage. On those occasions, he reminded me of a female llama who's been surprised in her bath.

But when the full panoply of the Allied invasion had gathered together at Normandy, I knew that the final victory would not be long in coming. It would not come without fearful loss of life, the most appalling destruction. But it did come. Europe was liberated; victory in the West was won. And I was absolutely spent, I admit it. Physically, mentally, emotionally.

(The sound of a quiet military drum-roll)

Yet even in the high jubilation of V-E Day - Victory in Europe - my mind turned to one who was not with us, save in spirit. Three weeks earlier, as the Allies were pouring across the Rhine, I received a phone call from Washington. I turned to Clemmie: "It's terrible news. The President of the United States is dead. Your friend and mine, Clemmie He died upon the wings of victory. But he saw those wings ...and he heard them beating."

(Getting his coat, CHURCHILL sits to the left of the table)

The end of the war in Europe meant the end of our coalition government. There had to be a new election. The night before the ballot, I had a dream. I was on an operating table. A white sheet had been pulled over me, and I was being wheeled away. That's not to say that I expected to lose. When the results were announced, they struck like a physical blow. Clemmie said "Now Winston, this may be a blessing in disguise." I said "Well if so, my dear, right now it's quite effectively disguised." The new prime minister is a Mr. Clement Attlee, a man I've known a long time. A modest man with much to be modest about.

There were calls for my retirement. The editor of the Times wrote that I should, in his words, "...retire gracefully." I replied "I leave when the pub closes!"

The King wanted to make me a Knight of the Garter. I said "With the greatest respect, your Majesty, how could I accept the Order of the Garter, when your people have already given me the order of the boot?"

My doctors prescribed for me a regimen of rest and exercise. I said "I got my exercise by being a pallbearer to those of my friends who believed in regular running and calisthenics!"

I did take a painting vacation in Italy. It was joyous to be at peace again with Italians. And it was while I was there - as the final peace accords were being signed with the Japanese aboard your battleship Missouri - that I received an invitation to speak in Missouri. At Westminster College in Fulton. Now I didn't recognize the college, although 'Westminster' is not an unfamiliar name to me. But I did recognize the signature at the end of the postscript: "Come. And I'll introduce you. Harry Truman." I couldn't let an opportunity like this go by. Plus, it was work -- what a joy! I arrived in Washington with my speech fully prepared.

At Union Station, I met President Truman aboard the Presidential train that was to take us to Fulton. The first thing he did was to show me the new Presidential seal that he just redesigned. He explained that the seal goes everywhere the President goes. It must be displayed on every lecturn. He said "I have redesigned it so that the eagle - instead of facing the arrows, he now faces the olive branches. What do you think?" I said "Mr. President, I would prefer the American eagle's neck to be on a swivel, so that he might face the arrows or the olive branches, as the occasion might demand." I believe I put the President aback just a bit. He finally said "Well, how 'bout some whiskey." And I thought that a capital idea! Then they brought out a bottle of Old Grandad. I said "No, that's not whiskey, that's bourbon." I pulled the switch at Silver Spring, Maryland, and lo and behold, a case of Johnnie Walker Black Label was brought to the rescue.

(Pours himself a drink)

I've always taken more out of alcohol than alcohol's taken out of me, you know. I had my first dram of whiskey as a young lieutenant. In India, the local water was unfit to drink. We had to add whiskey to make it safe. And through diligent effort, I learned to like it. Cheers!

We also played poker on that trip. I was no expert, although I knew the game and its various forms. The spirits, both liquid and ethereal, offered such enjoyment that I actually said to the President of the United States "Mr. President, when we play poker, I think I will call you Harry." The President said "Well, all right, Winston."

So, fortified by the company I was keeping, by what you call Scotch, what we call whiskey, I returned to work on my speech in the privacy of my own compartment. I opened up a map of Europe, and with my ink pen, I drew a line. From Poland

CHURCHILL   55

in the north to the Adriatic in the south.
I contemplated that malignant line. Next
morning, at Westminster College in Fulton,
I came to the crux of what I wanted to say:

"From Stettin in the Baltic to Trieste in
the Adriatic, an iron curtain has descended
across the continent..."

Iron curtain - that was the phrase the press
picked up, and it was not in the original text.
You see, there were some things I wanted to
warn you about. I see a world increasingly
divided. Remember that line? On our side,
the people own the governments. On their
side, the governments own the people.

(The sound of a drum)

Twice in my lifetime, the long arm of
destiny has reached out across the seas and
involved the entire life and manner of the
United States in a struggle. There's no use
your saying "We don't like it, we don't
want it, our forefathers left Europe to avoid
these quarrels". The people of the United
States cannot escape world responsibility.
But no one doubts the capacity of the
United States to respond in a deadly crisis.
The real test of leadership - and that is
what you are, leaders of the free world –
the real test is not the sudden tug of an

emergency, but the steady pull over the long haul. There never was a war in all history easier to avoid than the one that has just devastated vast areas of the globe. We surely must not let it happen again.

(The drumming ends)

And you keep this close to your hearts. In this year and in all years to come, knowing where we stand and all there is still to do, let the sun shine on both sides of the Iron Curtain. For the sun ever be equal on both sides, the Curtain will be no more. Such is my faith in God and in humanity.

These days, I am often asked about the future - my future. I realize that I have more years behind me than ahead of me. But I always say that when the time arrives, I'm ready to meet my Maker. Whether my Maker is prepared for the great ordeal of meeting me is another matter.

(CHURCHILL crosses to the righthand chair and sits) I was with my friend and scientific advisor Professor Lindemann just the other day. We were sitting in one of the saloons of the great Savoy Hotel in London. As I regarded my brandy glass I said to him "Freddy, tell me. If all the wine, whiskey, cognac and champagne that I've enjoyed

in all my lifetime were to be poured into this saloon... would it fill up the room?" The Prof pulled out his slide rule, made his computations and said "Winston, if all the alcohol you've consumed in your lifetime were to be poured into this chamber, then I predict that the liquid level would rise approximately to your nose." Well, I regarded the vast space between myself and the ceiling and contemplated my "advancing" years. And I said "How much is still to do; how little time to do it!"

(The sound of Big Ben tolling twelve. The following speech is timed to bells as CHURCHILL goes to get cigar, looking up)

You know, there would be no purpose in living when there is nothing to do, and I like things to happen.

(Slow cross to easel)

If they don't happen, I like to make them happen. You never know what's going to happen next. Such is life with its twists and turns. It's a strange riddle. The struggles, the labour, the constant rush of affairs, the sacrifice of so many things...and for what?

(Bells end)

Well for me, when I get to heaven, I intend

to spend a large portion of my first million years painting. I so mean to get to the bottom of the subject.

(Lights fade as CHURCHILL smiles as he begins to paint. Slow BLACKOUT)

END OF PLAY

ABOUT CHURCHILL

WINSTON CHURCHILL (1874-1965), often acclaimed the greatest British citizen of the 20th century, was a Renaissance man of high accomplishment – author, statesman, writer and historian, inventor, military hero and prime minister of Great Britain twice. He is credited, along with FDR, for leading the Allied victory over Hitler and the Axis during World War II. Among his many honors, Mr. Churchill won the Nobel Prize for literature in 1953 and was made an honorary citizen of the United States in 1962. He wrote over forty books and saw endless collections of his speeches published during his lifetime. He also was a respected painter, creating over 400 canvases from his beginnings as an artist in 1914. Winston Churchill died on January 24, 1965 at ninety years of age – exactly seventy years to the date of his father's passing...as he himself predicted.

ABOUT THE PLAYWRIGHT

RONALD KEATON, a native Hoosier, is an actor/writer/singer based in Chicago. He has extensive professional experience in the city's theatres, as well as in regional theatre. His versatility as a performer extends from Shakespeare (TWELFTH NIGHT, AS YOU LIKE IT, JULIUS CAESAR, THE MERCHANT OF VENICE, among others) to musical theatre (1776, GUYS AND DOLLS, THE MUSIC MAN, BIG RIVER, et al) and much inbetween. Mr. Keaton offers television, voiceover and narration work, recently completing an acclaimed documentary on the Indiana poet James Whitcomb Riley. He also has two other solo pieces, IN HEAVENLY PEACE and WHISPERS FROM THE MOON, a solo musical with composer William Underwood.

SORDELET
ink

NOVELS

THE STAR-CROSS'D SERIES
THE MASTER OF VERONA BY DAVID BLIXT
VOICE OF THE FALCONER BY DAVID BLIXT
FORTUNE'S FOOL BY DAVID BLIXT
THE PRINCE'S DOOM BY DAVID BLIXT
VARNISH'D FACES: STAR-CROSS'D SHORT STORIES BY DAVID BLIXT

WILL & KIT
HER MAJESTY'S WILL BY DAVID BLIXT

THE COLOSSUS SERIES
COLOSSUS: STONE & STEEL BY DAVID BLIXT
COLOSSUS: THE FOUR EMPERORS BY DAVID BLIXT

PLAYSCRIPTS

ALL CHILDISH THINGS BY JOSEPH ZETTELMAIER
CHURCHILL BY RONALD KEATON
THE COUNT OF MONTE CRISTO ADAPTED BY CHRISTOPHER M WALSH
DEAD MAN'S SHOES BY JOSEPH ZETTELMAIER
THE DECADE DANCE BY JOSEPH ZETTELMAIER
EBENEEZER: A CHRISTMAS PLAY BY JOSEPH ZETTELMAIER
EVE OF IDES - A PLAY BY DAVID BLIXT
THE GRAVEDIGGER: A FRANKENSTEIN PLAY BY JOSEPH ZETTELMAIER
HATFIELD & McCOY BY SHAWN PFAUTSCH
HER MAJESTY'S WILL ADAPTED BY ROBERT KAUZLARIC
IT CAME FROM MARS BY JOSEPH ZETTELMAIER
THE MOONSTONE ADAPTED BY ROBERT KAUZLARIC
NORTHERN AGGRESSION BY JOSEPH ZETTELMAIER
ONCE A PONZI TIME BY JOE FOUST
THE RENAISSANCE MAN BY JOSEPH ZETTELMAIER
THE SCULLERY MAID BY JOSEPH ZETTELMAIER
SEASON ON THE LINE BY SHAWN PFAUTSCH
STAGE FRIGHT: A HORROR ANTHOLOGY BY JOSEPH ZETTELMAIER
A TALE OF TWO CITIES ADAPTED BY CHRISTOPHER M WALSH

ESSAYS

ORIGIN OF THE FEUD BY DAVID BLIXT
TOMORROW & TOMORROW BY DAVID AND JANICE L BLIXT

WWW.SORDELETINK.COM